SADIE
AND
LEXIE

Written by   Nancy Zimmerman
Illustrated by   Rebekah Raffield

Book 1 in Sadie's Great Adventures

Dedicated to Sadie Callan

HEDGEHOG HILL PRESS

An imprint of S & Z Unlimited, LLC

S & Z Unlimited

P.O. Box 2380

Anderson, IN 46018

Sandzunlimited.com

A Hedgehog Hill Press original, 2016

ISBN: 978-0692682111

SADIE

AND

LEXIE

Once upon a time, there was a young girl named Sadie. Sadie lived in Scotland.

She lived in the country with her mother, father, and grandfather. Sadie was 8 years old and she was looking forward to summer vacation……. kind of. You see, Sadie didn't have any brothers or sisters and none of her friends lived near her. She had no one to play with.

Sadie's grandfather enjoyed fishing

and he would take Sadie with him on

lovely Saturday afternoons. She enjoyed

the time she spent with her grandfather

and he taught her all about nature. He

pointed out different birds and before

long, she was able to know what kinds of

birds were around her just by listening to

their voices. It was fun to spend time

with him and she enjoyed it even more

when he let her help catch fish.

Sadie enjoyed helping her mother prepare dinner in the evening.

Sometimes her mother would let her help bake a cake to have for dessert. Sadie loved cake, especially chocolate cake.

After the meal was over, Sadie would help her mother clear the table and wash the dishes. Sadie was a good helper.

Sadie enjoyed reading and she would spend her time in the evenings looking at books or playing puzzles. Sometimes she would watch television.

Sadie enjoyed these times at home with her parents and her grandfather, but she secretly wished there was someone her age for her to play with.

When bedtime came, her mother would come to tuck her in for the night.

Sadie's father like to work with wood in his spare time. He would let Sadie come to his shop and pick out pieces of wood for him to cut into pieces that could be put together to make birdhouses.

He would let Sadie help him put the birdhouses together and paint them. Sometimes she would paint plain birdhouses and sometimes she and her father would paint magical looking

birdhouses in bright colors.

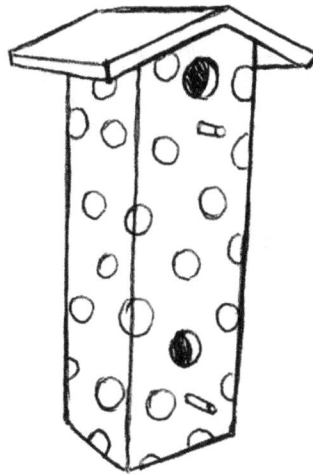

On Saturdays, he and Sadie would take them to the Farmer's Market and sell them.

They made different houses for different birds. Sadie learned that each kind of bird needed a different kind of house.

If the bird was little, it needed a small hole so that it could get in but other bigger birds could not get into it to

disturb their eggs.

Sadie enjoyed going to the Farmer's Market because there were all sorts of booths there.

She would talk her father into buying fudge from one person and a pretty bracelet for her mother from another person.

Sadie would see some of her friends there too and there would be time for them to visit before she had to return

home.

When Sadie got home she gave her mother the bracelet that she and her father had picked out. Her mother was surprised and really liked it. She gave Sadie a big hug.

Sadie got a piece of fudge out of the box, put it on a small plate, and took it into the living room to give to her grandfather. He thanked Sadie and gave her a hug too. He bit into it and said,

"Yum. This is good."   Sadie smiled.

Sadie went to bed that night and was looking out her bedroom window. She saw lots of stars in the night sky. They were so pretty. All of a sudden, there was a streak where a star was falling.

Sadie knew it was really what happened when a meteor, or a piece of a rocky object in space that burns as it falls to the earth. She liked calling it falling star because she could always

make a wish on a falling star.

Sadie took a breath and made her wish that night. She was excited that she had seen the falling star because she knew exactly what she would wish for.

She could hardly wait to get to sleep because the sooner she slept, the sooner tomorrow would come and maybe her wish would come true.

She wrapped her arm around her little

white stuffed dog and before long her

eyes got heavy and she went to sleep.

The next morning Sadie bounced out

of bed and got dressed quickly. She went

down to the kitchen where her mother

was fixing breakfast. They were having

bacon and eggs. Sadie got to put the

bread in the toaster and pour the orange

juice.

After breakfast, Sadie asked if she

could go back into the woods behind the

house and play for a while. Her parents

said it was okay if she would be careful.

Sadie enjoyed walking in the woods.

She would always find interesting things

in her walks. Sometimes she found an

interesting shaped twig or branch.

Sometimes she found pretty leaves.

There were always pretty flowers in

bloom. One time she found a very smooth

rock that was kind of shaped like a heart.

She had taken it home and painted it.

She gave it to her mother for her

birthday last year.

Sadie was looking at a leaf when she heard a sound. She looked around but she couldn't see where the noise was coming from.

She went deeper into the woods and got closer to the sound. It was a sad sound, kind of like a baby crying. Sadie knew it couldn't be a baby in the woods but she was curious about what it was.

She was kind of scared but she kept

looking.

She looked over and saw something move. She slowly walked over to the place where she had seen movement.

All of a sudden, something ran toward her and she screamed. She started to run away and fell.

The little animal stopped and slowed down. Sadie looked up with tears in her eyes. She had hurt her foot and she was scared until she saw two little button

eyes looking back at her.

Her wish had come true. She had wished the night before that she had a friend to play with.

Here in the woods was a lost puppy. The puppy came closer to her as she held her hand out to pet it. The puppy wiggled and wagged its tail.

Finally the puppy came close enough to let Sadie pet it. The puppy was dirty and looked hungry. Sadie would take it home

and feed it then give it a bath.

Sadie got up and limped out of the woods. She got to her back yard and her mother was coming out of the house.

"Mother," Sadie shouted, "Look what I found in the woods. Can I keep it?"

Sadie's mother said, "It isn't yours, Sadie. This dog might have a little boy or girl looking for it. We need to try and find its owners."

Sadie put her head down and tried not to cry. She loved the little dog.

Sadie's parents went to all of the neighbor's houses to try and find the dog's owners but no one stepped up to claim the dog.

They told Sadie that it was a very big responsibility to have a pet. They wanted to make sure she was ready to take care of the little pup that she had named, Lexie.

She listened to her parents as she sat

at the kitchen table petting Lexie.

The next day, Sadie went to her piggy bank and got some of the money out so her father could take her to town to buy some things the puppy would need like a comfortable cushion to be her bed.

Sadie's parents let Lexie sleep in Sadie's room on her own bed. Sadie didn't tell them that Lexie would get in bed with her.

Sadie and Lexie were so happy that they had found each other to play with.

Author's Notes

This is the first of a series of books for children aged 3-8. It is our hope that you and your child will enjoy coloring the illustrations as you talk about what is happening in Sadie's life.

We have included information about "falling stars" and also about birdhouses. Feel free to explore both of these topics with your child. You can also discuss outdoor findings on walks in the woods

and taking care of pets and the

importance of being a good pet owner.

Feel free to get in touch with us at

info@sandzunlimited.com for any imput

or suggestions of "Great Adventures" in

the future. Include your child's ideas. It

is never too early to include them in an

imaginative discussion of books.

You can color with your child and

discuss many of these events in your life

and share memories.

Enjoy,

Nancy Zimmerman and

Rebekah Raffield